About th

Janet Lees is a poet and artist based in the Isle of Man, where her mother's family comes from. In 2018 she was selected as the artist to represent the island at the Festival Interceltique in Lorient, France, with an exhibition of art photography, poetry and film. Her poetry has been widely published in journals and anthologies around the world, and her film-based works selected for international prizes and festivals including the Aesthetica Art Prize and Filmpoem. She holds an MA in Creative Writing from the University of Lancaster, and a BA Hons in Creative Arts from Manchester Metropolitan University. This is her first book.

This publication has been supported by Culture Vannin

Lily Publications Ltd
PO Box 33, Ramsey, Isle of Man, British Isles
Tel: +44 (0) 1624 898446
Fax: +44 (0) 1624 898449
www: lilypublications.co.uk

for Ian

'For whatever we lose (like a you or a me)
it's always ourselves we find in the sea.'

e.e. cummings

Design & typography by Ian Pilbeam

Contents

Mapping Hi-Zex Island

On the first day
we viewed the island from above:
a lightning flower flung across the skin of the sea
under the burning eye of the sun.

On the second day, we approached it from the water,
observing aspects of permanence –
three years and four months an island now,
its shape shifting between evening and morning.

On the third day we walked it, measured its synthetic
drumlins, its rope beaches, its tightly woven coves,
weighed the miles of clouded water beneath our feet.
Earth of a kind. Sea of a kind.

On the fourth day we went down to meet
this land mass in its own twilight. Ghost nets reached out
to finger our hair, calling us to the mausoleum
of the island's rusted underbelly.

On the fifth day, we saw the ocean swarm –
angelfish and rainbow runners twisting through drifts
of polymer confetti that playact as food,
feeding the very body of our island.

The sixth day we spent logging life.
A shore crab. Clams. An albatross in flight
off the western peninsular. We collected old eel traps,
scraps like pastel coloured sharks' teeth

with which to make a necklace for the children.
We bowed our heads under the weight of that night's stars.
And when the seventh dawn came,
we saw our work was done.

Discovered by Captain Charles Moore, Hi-Zex Island is made up of fishing gear, nets and buoys believed to have come from the 2011 tsunami that devastated parts of Japan.

Practising

She is in her bedroom practising piano. On the wall above the piano is the picture that gets put up every year – the manger scene with Mary in a cloak of the most beautiful blue. The blue is still beautiful even though the wonder of the picture has faded. In her head she is in the telephone box. It is its own muzzled universe. Steamed-up windows, vicious little paint flakes, a hollow metal smell mixed with piss and dead cigarettes. The clammy black receiver, mouthpiece peppered with tiny holes. She imagines her voice going into the holes, splitting into bright streamers of sound in the darkness behind them, her message exactly as she wishes it to be for a shining moment, then sucked thin into the curly cord and pulled blindly through the telegraph wires by the world's most powerful magnet that is the listener, into whose ear she tumbles muddy and squashed, the colour of plasticine all mixed together. She hits the cracked B flat above middle C. Then she is back in the box, fingers tangled in the empty cord, the pips in her ear like a lack of stars.

Bedtime

When I was eleven –
a ball of wildfire hissing at rules, lies,
cracks in the pavement, blurred desires –

they pinned me into the duvet
to starve my heart of air and light,
little knowing that inside I was water

compelled to run downhill towards
a huge man seen through trees at dusk,
as if he were my saviour.

Tonight, as I lie confined
to the same little place as yesterday,
he is running towards me.

I want to punch him
but I pray for him instead,
fill him up with holy smoke

until he falls down dead.
And now he walks again
into that Soho diner

with tangerine leather seats
and scorch marks on the walls.
He wants us to stay here

forever, he tells me,
picking burnt seeds out of his teeth,
sprinkling ashes into my cup

House of water

'The Depths of the Sea' by Edward Burne-Jones

He caught your untrained heart
the first time you watched him walk
the long white shore on his clever feet

and now you have caught him;
brought him, laid on the blade of your tail,
home to your house of water

washed him clean of his name
stroked away the sorrows
from his milk and butter skin

explained to him the secret ways of fish
and all the things you wish –
you, born of moonshine

blood part-brine part-stardust
daughter of the world's misfortune –
your whole body singing *all mine all mine*

blind to his closed eyes
his salted lips
his silent heart.

Yours to keep. So bury him deep
in your bed of fool's gold
until he turns to water too

then drink him down and dream his tread
and rise to walk the sleepless shore
on dumbstruck feet

each step more painful than the last;
condemned to live as flesh and blood
when all you wanted was to love.

We two girls together singing

Inspired by 'A Young Lady's Adventure' by Paul Klee
After David Hockney and Walt Whitman

I am
drawn in
to your adventure;
its signature scent
of line-dried hope-white linen
cut with black coffee
and frosted city air,
velvet growl of French cigarettes
rising up from pumping bass notes
of undiluted girlblood;
the skin-tight harmony of our raw code
tripping off our tongues of gold lamé.
Two maids
unmade,
holding a bag of sky behind our backs,
laughing, stealing, slashing, burning,
catwalking the canyons of every next yearning,
our stormforce heartbeat scrawled across the night.
Me-you, free and fluid,
doing the bump with each new moon,
wrapped in clouds of our own breath
and the ghosts we can't see yet –
treading the dusk above our heads, offering
our hearts in their outstretched hands –
as a spiral staircase builds itself around our legs
and goat-eyed birds put their beaks to our necks
and the grinning lizard runs ahead,
its tiny crown flashing in the light
from our unquenchable momentary blaze.

Rags and bones

I have hung out my clothes
on the washing line at the edge of the world.
Silhouetted arms and legs
give dumbstruck kicks and jerks,
stiff with salt and too much mending
by hands that have lost
the scent of naked,
eyes that can't see
to thread a needle.

Today I have a glass head

I woke up to its rainbows on the wall.
My fingers trembled over its vitrified
contours; I pictured it revolving on a plinth,
filling showgoers with iced fire.

But when I looked in the mirror
my head's guts glared back – stained
glass veins, frozen tripe of brain
and all my snake-pit thoughts.

Out in the world, the shame of it burns –
a hat is not much use when your face
gives everything away. My collarbone
chafes, a razor shell rack from which

the rest of me hangs like something flayed –
as if my own cold mouth has consumed
the skin to bring on full body glassification.
The notion sparks outrage in passersby

whose eyes track my mind as it runs for cover
headlong to the river's disinterested murk,
its irresistible suck like birth in reverse.
Better that than the sudden shatter,

iridescent matter among hurrying feet;
my head swept up and shipped far east,
melted down for a wine bottle
or a string of cheap beads.

There is something wrong with her heart

In the dream it's an egg,
ringing like an alarm clock

which turns into an engine
that the doctor tries to jump-start.

He is dressed in blue overalls
and looks like Jesus –

the Kwik Fit guy
playing a part.

ranslation
ıg lost.
L.51

Space junk

'And do you think people are talking
about you on the TV?' I croak 'No',
throat stripped by the grey snake they sent
down to suck the deathwish out of me.
He could be a newsreader, this ironic doctor
shielded by a desk; frost moustache aligned
with postbox mouth. Red when shut,
black when open. Reflecting my spectrum.
A gnarled part of me wants to ram
something too big in that black hole
and watch it fill with red. But more of me
is carried on Valium contrails, ghosted out
against a veil of dead stars that still shine.
'And do you think the washing machine
is a spaceship?' I wish I did think that.
I think I could be one myself –
a metal vessel spun across the universe,
burning up on this re-entry.

Unnamed

At these times
these hunger moon times

you come keening
through the squall

Insistent wanting   swaddled
in snowy white noise

A half curled hand
a simple plan

to drag my black heart
back to bedlam

Bluebeard, beachcombed

After Clarissa Pinkola Estés

Out walking on the shore
at the headland of unsound mind
you come upon a scrap of him
masquerading as a chopped
hank of fisherman's rope —
sky blue frayed   slightly faded
but clearly identifiable
as a six-inch length
of the devil's work
You picture it stripped
from his stone-cold chin —
the bone beneath hard as gneiss
and twice as old —
twisted into a token
of his plummet into you —
a gannet dive at nightfall
designed to cleave
your heart in two
so quick and clean
it might have gone unnoticed
but for the sharp eyes of your sisters
thanks to whom there's no sign now
of the key that won't stop bleeding —
but then again
it's dark down there
at the bottom of the deep blue sea

Ld.
Laugh out loud

Unmanned

5 am
and
I am
the buried
moon in the
black nail of the
broken little toe on the
third foot of the creature that howls
Whichever way you throw me I will stand.

Housework

You told me to go inside
So I went inside
Broke through the pelvis

with that heavy tool
my father's dentist liked to use
Climbed the ladder of the spine up to

a nameless servant's room
where leaves and soft rain have stolen in
through holes the mice have made

I turned the old things over
with a plastic spade – the exact same colour
my mother's lips turned nine months back

so that you can say
what is treasure what is trash
while I pretend to play

with my sister's Fisher Price castle
filling the moat
from a cut on my thumb

shaking the tiny fist of myself
at the flat-pack world
unmade, outside

Things had a way of disappearing in the garden

Coins, china,
boiled sweets,
secrets.

A portrait of St Peter.
A child singing.
Everything, stolen.

My heart lost
in the mist
for days at a time.

Love. Missing
for so long, when it came
it was just

strange –
a disconcerting carousel;
just some kind of

waiting
room
at the bottom of the garden

Resort

In the dark months the sea shows its hand,
dumping stones as big as cannonballs
at the doors of The Trafalgar.

Inside, a fibreglass Viking
guards the flat screen TV
and Ida Kelly leads a sing-song

on her squeezebox – a gift
from the last accordion factory in France.
Less than half your blood belongs here.

Past and future run through you
like blurred words in seaside rock.
Every August you drown

in carnival crowds that disperse at dusk
leaving you washed up before
a Punch & Judy stall on the beach.

Looking out past its candy-stripe curtains,
you watch the fins of a basking shark glide by,
pointing towards other bodies of land.

The eye of the storm

She stepped into my room
wearing nothing but a self-coloured tattoo,
a firework bloom thrown
over her body in skin filigree

It's a lightning flower, I said,
staring at roots snaking into the dark
half-moon of her waist. *I've seen pictures*
on the internet – and this is a dream

It's a tree, she breathed, quiet
as leaves falling on the knife edge of
November. *The last but one –*
and you're awake

Outer Hebrides

This land is dreaming
Wide awake
you try to fall

the long clean fall of faith
to feel the dream
through the blood in your feet

the buried moons
at the ends
of your fingers

the hinges
at the shoulder blades
that once had wings attached

But all you're getting
is tired grey fire
sluggish rills of something

that may or may
not be molten
a dusty obsidian

paperweight
in the shape
of a small still heart

Last night we were undressed by the wind

It took our shoes first;
we watched them rise like odd dense birds
into the indigo sky.

It undid buttons, habits, words;
twirled away the shadows on your face,
the lines engraved on mine.

It freed the magpie in your ribcage,
unzipped each one of my muttering scars,
opened our heads to the blazing dark.

And then there was only bright skin.
And then we were
just air

Last night we were undressed
by the wind. This morning
we woke in our clothes.

Waiting in the wings of England:

Wanlip, Warninglid,
Poverty Hill.

Destinations the map
mutters darkly over –

the hard-to-read small print
on what lies ahead

beyond rear windows filled
with sucker-footed soft toys

and electric pink signs
singing *Princess on Board.*

Cotgrave. Wideopen.
Gibbet Wood. Nomansland.

Marching backwards
into a monoculture of rape

spotted with poppies
and patrolled by crows

in their frayed City suits.
Watching. Reckoning. Waiting.

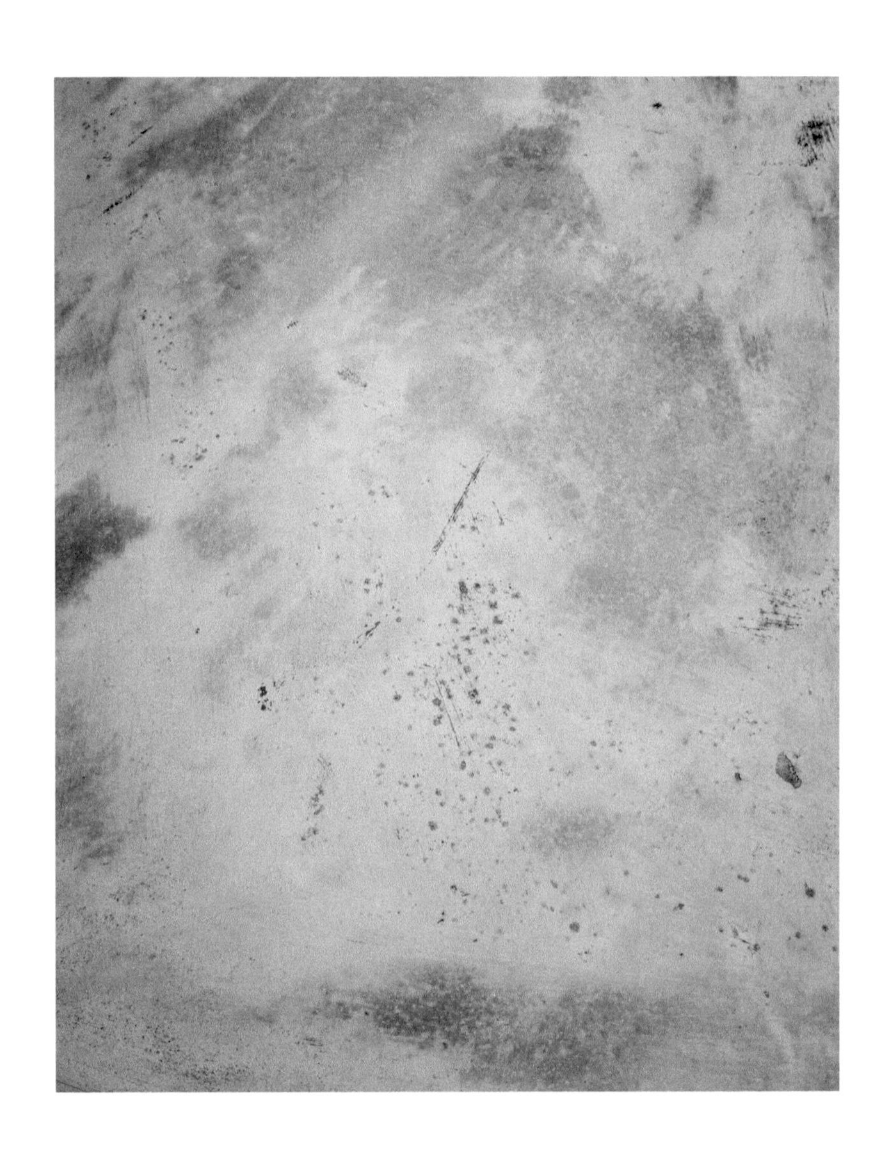

Reconsecrated

A taste of you slipped into me
like moonlight in a locked church.
The flesh at first left me cold:
respectful fingers, diffident lips
spilling awkward mumbles in
The Angel's fug. We hunted down
politeness with iced vodka
and flew outside, where the night
took your tongue and gave it to mine,
igniting a flame that swallowed
Soho's oxygen whole to shape
the way I kissed you back:
adoration of seventeen again,
ablaze with the lost conviction
that this can be a state of grace,
this immaculate need to fuck in the street.

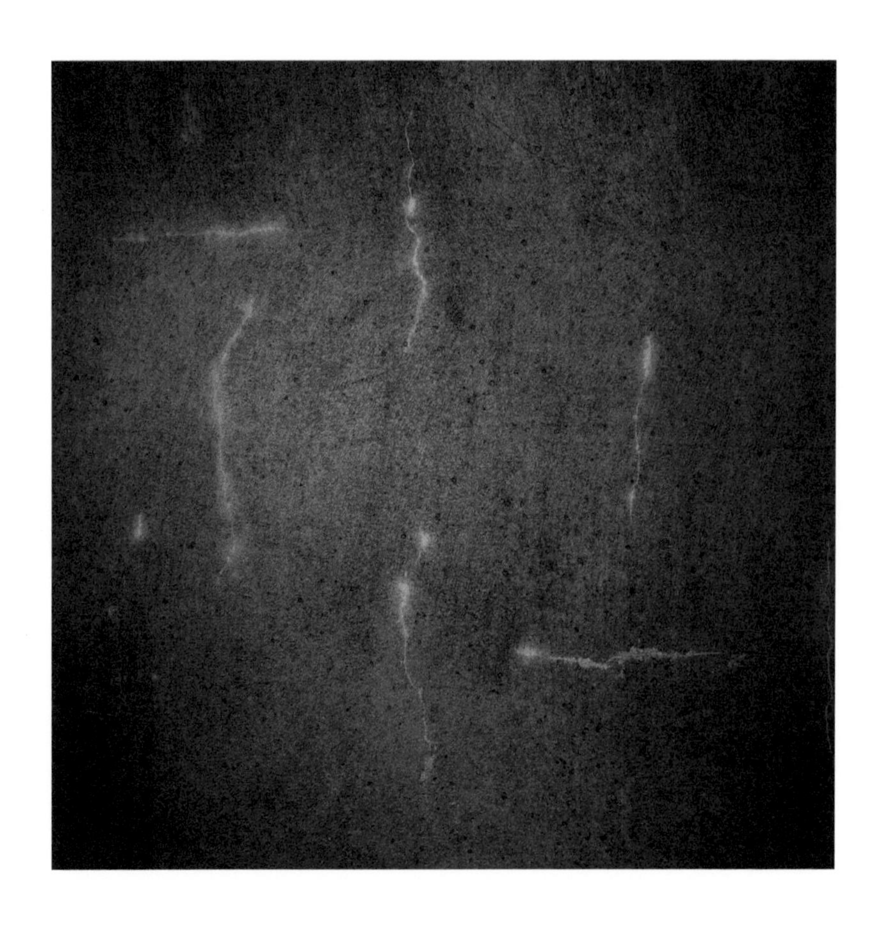

Catching fire

You said
from behind your book of shapes
If a fire got in that would be it   whoosh
and I nodded abstractedly
not thinking it through
the patient touch paper   the incendiary itch
the virgin tongue that licks along the heartlines on each palm
twists in
through an undefended edge
and then
the blood orange bristle of indoor fire
my fingers burning holes in everything
curtains   soft furnishings   pelts
the bone dry roses of that bouquet   that bunch of old pursed mouths
gone   *whoosh*
in a tangerine flash
the tendons in their carping throats turned sparks that fountain up
to singe the cooling skin of last night's moon
rain down to feed a fire that eats the parquet floor for breakfast
blows open doors with a *BOOMBOOMBOOM*
makes every window sing a cracked tune
houses without chimneys should not huff and puff
fetches us out of our little cold stoves
to fill us with a roman candle rush
that boils my blood like jubilee jam
and I am
in love with the act of making fire
my cape of smoke
this newborn burn
the tinder
and flint
of each
next
word

Indelible

You cracked me
like a book too tightly bound

just wide enough to read
the cyphered part

that spoke to you
that let your fingers in

to touch my paper heart
to write a kinder truth

It is said

They say it's going to snow tomorrow.
They say the glaciers are melting into the sea.
They say that blood is thicker than water,
that our bones can crumble into this reluctant river
as we age. They say that whispering your fears
into trees will take your fears away,
that today is a gift, death a release,
that the dead are smiling at us through the thinnest places –
our unlocked doors, unfallen tears, the emptiness
that makes up nearly all of every atom.
They say you learn to live alongside
these smiles you hardly ever see;
to smile back blind. They say *time heals.*
They say *just give it time.*

Saltwater

After Anne Morrow Lindbergh

Here are coquina shells,
        here are feather stars,
                white sand dollars, fragments
                of the bones of birds.
        Here is sea ivory, salt rose, thrift,
the flowers of the bruise of the shore.
Here is the paper nautilus,
        a cradle for your heart;
                the wide open door
                of a channelled whelk,
        a moon shell emptied
of everything but patience.
Here are sharp flights,
        dark forests
                of dead man's bootlaces,
                dip and wheel and ragged tide wash
        of torn-to-pieces-hood.
Here is my cathedral.
Here is your horizon–
        a straight bite of wilderness
                reflected in the pupil of the eye.
                Here is the milk of saltwater,
        cloud. Here is rainwater
carrying dust. Here is life.
Here is daughter, sister, wife,
        the turning point of the tide of thought;
                here is white breath
                held
        by the sky;
the day's last sliver of pale lemon light.
Here you are,
        waking in the same small room as your sister:
                flying fish, shooting star–
                scattering light each side of the sunrise;
        lost to the water,
lost to the air

i.m. Carole Lees

Physic

The moon changes size
Tonight it is small and high
white and hard as a pill

While you dream of stone trees
under the ground
it drops

from the sky
into the glass beside your bed
dissolves with a bone-saw sigh

The water clouds and then clears
stands ready to turn your veins into vines
to take the edge off the world

Poetry films

Liminal
vimeo.com/313343270

The questions we all want answers to
vimeo.com/322435510

The girls
vimeo.com/312086825

Waiting for everything
vimeo.com/314030340

Six things I know
vimeo.com/326788560

The ghosts of all your certainties
vimeo.com/314306603

Acknowledgements

Thank you to Jackie, Geoff, Niki and Carole, and my whole extended family. Thank you to Jenn Ashworth, Paul Farley, George Green, Zoe Lambert, Usha Kishore, Graham Mort, Sarah Sibley and John Singleton, for your priceless help with my poetry. Thank you to all my friends, mentors, collaborators and fellow artists for your support, encouragement and inspiration, in particular Ariane Barua, Kim Bennett, Sharon Blackie, Dave Bonta, Janet Bridle, Martyn Cain, Heather Capps, Bridget Carter, Janine Cording, Sean Crossley, Chaitanya Jivan Das, Beth Espey, Christy DeHaven, Irene Eisler, Lucy English, Jane Farrington, Myra Gilbert, Eric Glitheroe, Natalie Gordon, Tony Gray, Jane Hall, Maria Helks, Sarah Hendy, Suzy Holland, Ian Joyce, Kate Kirk, Joanna Kitto, Tom Konyves, Pat Kramek, Leni Lewis, Heather Maund, Katy Mitchell, Jackie Morrey Grace, Marc Neys, Beth Orton, Pippa & Miles Pettit, Paul Raymond, Terry Rooney, Paul Salisbury, Hinke Schreuders, the fantastic Shutter Hub team, Preman Sotomayor, Hazel Teare, Christina Thatcher, Ben Thomas, Janet Tolan, Mike Wade, Chris Waller, Glenn Whorrall and Mel Wright. Thanks most of all to Ian Pilbeam, for everything.

Acknowledgements *continued*

Some of the poems in this collection have been previously published in the *Aesthetica Creative Writing Anthology*, *Anomalie* magazine, *Artemis Poetry* magazine, BBC Radio's *Poetry Postcards* project, the *Climate Minds* anthology, *Earthlines* magazine, *Fanfare: an anthology of contemporary women's poetry*, *Lighthouse* magazine, the *Milestones* anthology, *Mill: the Templar anthology 2015*, *The Transnational* magazine, and *The Missing Slate.*

Some of the images have featured in the exhibitions *EuroCeltic Art* (Lorient, France, 2018), *Evidence of Humanity* (solo show, Isle of Man, 2018) *Out of the Ordinary* (London, 2018), and *Everything I Ever Learnt* (Cambridge, 2019). Grateful thanks to everyone involved.

janetlees.weebly.com

vimeo.com/janetlees

Instagram: @janetlees2001